Survival Fun

© 2004 **Pacific Learning**
© 2004 Written by **Anna-Maria Crum**
Edited by **Rebecca McEwen**
Designed by **Anna-Maria Crum**
Photography: Rod Bunn (cover); anthroarcheart.org (pp. 3, 16, 17 [top]); Getty Editorial (pp. 4, 5 [bottom], 6, 7, 8, 9, 10, 11 [bottom], 12, 13, 14 [top], 15, 17 [bottom], 18, 20, 21, 22, 23, 24, 25, 26 [bottom], 27, 29, 30); The Bridgeman Art Library/Getty Images (p. 5); North Wind Picture Archives (p. 11 [top]); Library of Congress (pp. 14 [bottom], 19 [top and center]); Denver Public Library (pp. 19 [bottom], 26 [top]); Rebecca McEwen (p. 28).

All rights reserved. No part of this publication may be reproduced or transmitted in any form or by any means, electronic or mechanical, including photocopying, recording, taping, or any information storage and retrieval system, without permission in writing from the publisher.

10 9 8 7 6 5 4 3

Published by
Pacific Learning
P.O. Box 2723
Huntington Beach, CA 92647-0723
www.pacificlearning.com

ISBN: 1-59055-466-3
PL-7623

Printed in China.

Contents

Skills to Survive	4
The Hunt Is On	6
On Horseback	10
Sports, of Course	14
Out in the Cold	18
Say It with Music	22
The Language of Life	28
Conclusion	30
Glossary	31
Index	32

Ceremonial skull ball detail from Chichen Itza

Skills to Survive

Catch a fish or go hungry. Run because your life depends on it. Build a fire or freeze to death. Could you survive in a world that demanded these things?

Today, many people hunt and fish for relaxation. Some run for exercise, relaxation, and sports events. Others ride horses for enjoyment and competition. Many of the things that people do for fun today were necessary skills thousands of years ago. If people couldn't hunt or fish, they might starve, especially in the winter when **edible** plants are few. Running might save a person's life if a wild animal or an enemy were in pursuit. Riding horses made it easier to cover vast lands in order to follow **migrating** herds.

Although most people no longer need these skills to survive, many still enjoy their modern-day variations. Now people simply enjoy the thrill of riding a horse, or the beauty of nature while fishing, or the freedom of running.

Anglers use light, flexible rods and colorful **flies** to attract trout in fast-moving mountain streams.

FISHING

This painting shows an Egyptian fishing scene.

Wall paintings in tombs show ancient Egyptians fishing with rods, nets, and spears. The ancient Greeks and Romans made flies of colorful feathers to attract fish. There are two kinds of modern fishing: commercial and sport. Sport fishing uses the same basic tools and techniques as early anglers. People make flies out of feathers and fish with rods, spears, and nets. One big difference between past and present is the popularity of catch-and-release fishing. Instead of keeping the catch, the fish are returned to the river or lake immediately after being caught.

Commercial fishing changed with engine-powered fishing boats. Fishing **trawlers** lay down huge nets. Then the boats drag the nets for miles until powerful winches pull them in, capturing thousands of pounds of fish. Because so many fish are caught at once, many parts of the world's oceans are overfished. The large fishing nets don't just catch fish, either. Sea turtles and ocean mammals such as dolphins drown if they are caught in the nets with the fish they are chasing for their own meal.

Large fishing boats have changed the nature of fishing. These boats can go into deep water and catch hundreds of thousands of fish at a time.

The Hunt Is On

For millions of years, our human ancestors developed and then perfected hunting skills. Sometimes, early people had their greatest success when they trapped animals. Other times, they stampeded animals over the sides of a cliff as a hunting strategy.

Over the years, humans learned to make hunting tools such as spears.

This ancient cave painting discovered in France shows people hunting a large, bisonlike animal.

Little by little, people gained new ways of hunting the food they needed to stay alive.

FALCONRY

More than 4,000 years ago, people in China used falcons to hunt small animals and birds. The falcons were trained to fly from the arm of their handler, chase down their prey, and fly back with the prey they had just killed. The sport of **falconry**, which includes other raptors such as eagles and hawks, was also popular in India and the Middle East.

Some people still raise falcons in Asia, but today this is for sport, not survival.

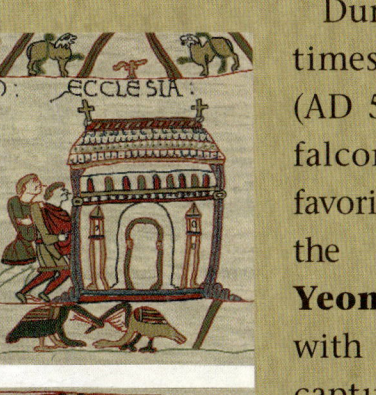

During medieval times in Europe (AD 500 to 1500), falconry was a favorite pastime for the **aristocracy**. **Yeomen** hunted with goshawks to capture food to eat. Shakespeare put many falconry **metaphors** in his plays, for during his time the sport was as popular as football is today.

People still practice falconry all over the world. In the United States a person has to have a special license to own a raptor. In order to get a license, each person has to train under a **Master Falconer** and then take a test.

In Europe, falconry sometimes took on the feel of a festival, with many servants working to keep the nobles well fed and entertained while the raptors hunted.

7

ARCHERY

A spear is a great way to hunt a large animal without getting close enough to risk injury. A bow is better than a spear if a person is hunting animals in wooded areas. Archeologists have found evidence of early bows and arrows in Africa. These **artifacts** are about 50,000 years old.

The bow and arrow were also excellent weapons. Egyptian archers shot arrows from the back of light chariots during battles. Working together at high speeds, chariot drivers could **outflank** the enemy army and cause a lot of damage.

In 1066, during the Battle of Hastings in England, an arrow through the eye killed King Harold II. In 1100, King William II died from an arrow during a hunting trip. Some believe his brother, Henry I, had him murdered so he could have the throne. One hundred years later, Richard the Lion-hearted died of an infection from an arrow wound. Clearly, it was dangerous to be King of England and be around arrows!

In Japan, this modern-day Samurai warrior is displaying the skill of archery on horseback.

Using a bow and arrow takes both skill and strength.

Today, people still use archery in hunting and competition. Modern bows have sights for aiming and the arrows travel at 150-plus miles per hour (241 kph). Bow strings are made from Kevlar, which is the same material that is used in bulletproof vests.

Archery was also part of the early Olympic Games, then dropped because the rules varied so significantly from country to country. Finally a single set of rules was established, and in 1972 archery returned to the summer games.

King Henry I, who reigned from from 1100 to 1135, proclaimed that an archer was innocent of murder if he happened to kill a man during archery practice. He should have included hunting trips too!

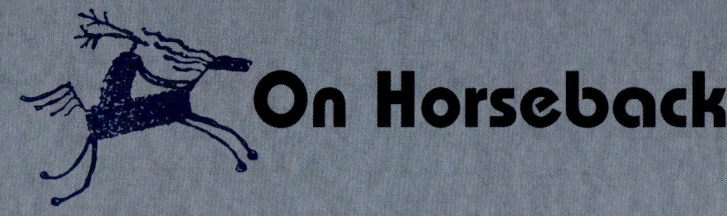

On Horseback

Long ago, horses were hunted as just another form of meat. Then, a few brave individuals figured out that they could gain speed and stamina by riding on a horse's back. There was no looking back – the course of human travel and trade changed forever.

As with all other survival skills, horseback riding has evolved a great deal from the early days. **Dressage** is a French word for "schooling of the horse," and it is a sport based entirely on the harmony between a horse and rider. The practice of fine-tuning riding skills dates back more than 2,000 years to ancient Greece.

Horses were specially trained to be flexible, calm, and supple, which is a great advantage in battle. A horse that panics could get its rider killed. The rider uses small body movements to signal the horse to move a specific way. The

The snowy white Lipizzan horses perform the highest level of dressage. Only the smartest and strongest horses are ever trained to do the "Airs Above the Ground" – three types of leaps originally used in battle.

capriole, which is a giant leap into the air, was an effective way to escape over the heads of the opposing infantry.

Today, dressage is a part of combined equestrian competitions that are called three-day events. The other two events are cross-country jumping and show jumping.

Some riders enjoy competitions that have a ranching heritage. Barrel racers, bareback riders, and calf-ropers all display skills that are needed to run a working cattle ranch.

Horses that were used in battle were trained to protect their riders before anything else – even if it meant sacrificing their own lives.

Anky van Grunsven (the Netherlands) won the gold medal for Dressage at the Sydney Olympics in 2000. Riding competitions are the only Olympic events in which men and women compete together.

POLO

Polo's roots go back to 600 BC. The name comes from the Tibetan word "pulu" which means "ball." This sport came to India and the Himalayas from Persia. The game builds both equestrian and military skills.

Next to actual battle, polo was the ultimate test of warriors. Like hockey on horseback, two teams of three or four players use a mallet to knock a wooden ball through the opponent's goal.

In early times players used the heads of sheep, goats, and other animals as the ball. Genghis Khan knocked his enemies' decapitated heads around the field. At the Persian court, the queen and her ladies-in-waiting also played.

Today, polo is popular all over the world. The field is 200 by 300 yards (183 by 275 m). The goal posts are made of a light material so they will break easily, just in case a horse crashes into one.

It can take several years to fully train a polo pony. The horse must be able to stop quickly, turn or twist, then resume running with little loss of speed. Think how difficult it can be to suddenly change direction while you are running and then suddenly start to run the opposite way. The horse has to be strong and agile to keep its balance while doing this. Plus, the horse must have the courage to bump into another horse upon its rider's command.

Modern-day polo

In Afghanistan, soldiers still play rough games of "no rules" polo.

When Alexander the Great ascended the throne in 336 BC, the Persian emperor, Darius III, sent him a polo ball and mallet saying he should stick to the game and leave war to the professionals. Alexander replied that the gift was symbolic, for he saw himself as the stick and the world as his ball. Since he went on to conquer most of the known world, including Darius's empire, no one can doubt who got the last laugh.

Sports, of Course

In ancient Greece, men, boys, and young girls could compete in Olympic events, but married women were forbidden to watch the games.

For thousands of years, sports have been a part of people's lives. Sometimes they are a training ground for battle, other times they are a form of exercise or a means to win a prize. In ancient times, the focus of competition was on an individual's ability to win.

This, however, was not the case in **Mesoamerica**. In this area of the world, men played team sports where the emphasis was on group strategy and cooperation.

We can see the influence of these early sports today. Team play, sports stadiums, standardized equipment, uniforms, protective gear, using a rubber ball, and in fact the very idea of professional players all started back in ancient times.

Baron Coubertin believed that France lost the Franco-Prussian War because the educational system did not supply the students with physical or spiritual strength. He devoted his life to improving physical fitness in schools, and in 1894 he organized the International Olympic Committee.

Watching the exceptional women athletes of today, it's hard to imagine that women were not allowed to compete until the 1900 Olympic Games in Paris, France.

OLYMPIC GAMES

The Olympic Games began in Greece more than 2,500 years ago. Every four years thousands of people came to the city of Olympia to watch athletes compete in different events. One legend says that in 720 BC an athlete named Orsippus lost his shorts in the middle of a race. He won anyway, and from then on male athletes competed nude.

The ancient games lasted 1,200 years until the Christian Roman emperor, Theodosius I, stopped them because of their pagan origins.

The modern Olympic Games started in 1896. Now the games open with a runner carrying a flaming torch lit in Olympia. The runner lights a cauldron in the Olympic stadium that burns for the duration of the games as a reminder of how it all began.

BALL GAMES

The first team sports started around 1600 BC in Mesoamerica. The Mesoamerican ball game was similar to soccer, for the players couldn't use their hands to hit or throw the hard rubber ball. Instead, a player had to use his elbows, knees, hips, foot, chest, or head to keep the ball moving and knock it through a stone hoop high on the wall of the playing field.

Players wore protective clothing, including knee and elbow pads and a wooden or leather yoke around the waist. By flicking their hips, the yoke would forcefully hit the ball. The ball varied in size and could weigh as much as eight pounds (3.6 kg). Some balls had a human skull in the center, which made it lighter and bouncier.

Players were often seriously injured and occasionally killed when the ball hit them in the wrong place.

Hitting the ball through the hole was so difficult, the first team to score a hoop won the game.

The Mesoamerican ball game had strong religious significance. In the Mayan version, the losing players had their hearts removed and their heads cut off as a sacrifice.

When Spanish invaders first saw the bouncing rubber ball in the Mesoamerican game, they thought it was magical, or perhaps even an instrument of the devil. Back then, rubber was completely unknown in Asia and Europe.

From Bladders to Footballs

Over in Europe during medieval times, people played games using an inflated pig or sheep's bladder as a ball. In the 1500s, the British invented football, which is the same game as soccer in the United States. American football started in 1869. The British and the Americans both still refer to the football as "the pigskin."

 Out in the Cold

Many early survival skills focused on how to live through the cold winter months.

Today, people still like to brave the raw winds and freezing temperatures, but now they do it for fun.

SKIING

A ski dating to 2500 BC found in a peat bog in Scandinavia is the earliest evidence of skiing. In prehistoric times people used skis to hunt game and gather food in the winter. Ancient people used skis to stay on top of the snow, not to go fast.

The military used skiing for troop movements and battle tactics, which ended up being largely responsible for the huge increase in skiing's popularity as a sport. During World War II, the U.S. Army's Tenth Mountain Division trained at Camp Hale in Colorado. Soldiers focused on learning rock climbing, skiing, and cold weather survival. Their skills led to several important victories in the mountains of Italy, which helped to end the war there.

It has only been in the last 200 years that people started skiing for fun. Now skis come in

a variety of shapes for all types of skiing – from the short freestyle skis to enormous long-jump skis.

SKATING

The oldest ice skates, found in the bottom of a Swiss lake, are almost 5,000 years old. Made from the leg bones of large animals, holes were bored at both ends to attach leather straps that tied on the skates.

"Schenkel" is Dutch for "skate" – it means "leg bone."

People used their skates to cross frozen lakes and canals in winter. Around AD 1500, the Dutch switched to metal runners. Speed skaters carried news from town to town.

In 1865, a man named Jackson Haines developed a new metal blade attached directly to his boot. He became famous for his jumps and spins. Later, he added a toe pick, which made new types of jumps possible. Modern figure skating was born.

Jackson Haines

After World War II, many of the U.S. Army Tenth Mountain Division veterans wanted to continue skiing. Their enthusiasm helped establish the ski industry in Colorado and Utah.

DOG SLEDDING

The toboggan, pulled by hand, was probably the first sleigh. Long, flexible, and narrow, these early sleds easily fit in the track left by snowshoes. They could carry a heavy load across a winter landscape.

Early inhabitants of the Arctic regions of Canada and Greenland used sleds they pulled by hand. Then, around AD 1500, a few people tried using dogs to pull the sleds. Since then, in one form or another, the **Inuit** have used dog sleds for transportation in the winter.

When prospectors and settlers arrived in the area, they copied the Inuit and used sleds to transport their goods. Dogs were expensive to buy and expensive to feed. A working sled dog can eat 5,000 to 8,000 calories a day. Compare that total to the recommended 2,900 calories a day for a human male!

The Iditarod is one of the most famous dog-sled races in the world. It commemorates a real event. In 1925, the people of Nome, Alaska, were hit by a diphtheria epidemic. Diphtheria is a sickness that causes a high fever and makes it difficult to breathe. Most people die from it.

The only medicine was in Anchorage, more than 1,150 miles (1,850 km) away. A train carried the medicine part of the way, then nineteen different dog sled teams took over the life-and-death relay race. They got the medicine there in time.

Dog sleds are built to glide over the top of wind-crusted snow.

The first roller-coaster was a block of ice. In fifteenth-century Russia, people climbed ice-covered mountain paths. At the top, they chiseled out blocks of ice, covered them with blankets, and rode them down the treeless trails. Later, people switched to sleds with runners, which were a little less painful to ride, and quite a bit faster. With the invention of railways it was a just a short loop-de-loop to roller-coasters!

Say It with Music

Music is a way for people to communicate as well as be entertained. Rituals and religious ceremonies also use music. It unites people because it appeals to their emotions. People who belong to the same country, religion, or cause are moved when they hear their **anthem**.

Throughout history, people have used music as a signal. Drumbeats can carry messages over very long distances. Imitating a certain birdcall might signal the **sentry** that a person is a friend, and should be allowed to pass.

INSTRUMENTS

Stone Age musicians played drums, rattles, and xylophones made from animal bones and skins. Wind instruments have a magical sound. Many tribal cultures believe the sound comes from the spirit world. The Kamayura Indians in the Brazilian rain forest worship their flutes, believing spirits live in them.

Drummers from New Guinea

Over the centuries, the military has used music in many ways. Soldiers marched to drumbeats. Bugles sounded the beginning of a battle, different maneuvers or plans during a battle, and then signaled a sad good-bye to anyone who died. Bagpipes stirred the blood and rallied the clans to battle. At one time, the English feared bagpipes so much they banned the Scots and the Irish from playing them.

Today, there are marching bands in parades or during halftime at a football game. The vibrations from these bands, or from any loud music, catches people up in the excitement of the beat.

The first bagpipes were played about 3,000 years ago in the Middle East. As the borders of their empire grew, Romans carried bagpipes with them on their conquests all the way to the British Isles. In this picture, famous rock musicians the Beatles add the bagpipes to their distinctive musical sound.

SINGING

It's impossible to know what singing was like during the Stone Age. It may have been just imitating animal calls and could even have started as a way to lure animals while hunting. The oldest song that anyone has ever heard of is a hymn for a Mesopotamian goddess. Even though this song is almost 3,500 years old, it uses the same seven-note scale we have today.

People sing for worship and for fun. They can sing with instruments or **a cappella**. They sing to entertain others, or by themselves. Even people who can't sing still sing, if only in the shower. It's part of human nature to express ourselves through song.

When rock and roll first came out, parents thought the music dangerous, and that it would corrupt their children. Radio stations banned the music in many areas, and "concerned citizens" burned the records.

Listen to modern music to find its historical roots. Can you hear yodeling in a hip-hop song?

YODELING

Yodeling is a kind of singing that started as a way to send messages from one neighbor to another – neighbors who lived on mountaintops, that is.

Yodelers break their voice during the call, and the sounds range from low-pitched notes to high ones. Yodels usually don't have words, and aren't really music. They are sound signals that can cover a great distance. It might be a cowherd calling another cowherd, or a woman calling her family home to dinner.

The first mention of the yodel comes from the Roman Emperor Julian in AD 4. He complained about the wild shrieking songs of the northern mountain people.

Yodeling isn't restricted to the Swiss Alps. Several African tribes yodel, including the forest pygmies. Even Tarzan yodeled his way through the stories about him.

Immigrants brought the yodel with them to the United States. The mixture of many cultures gave birth to yodeling heard in some bluegrass and country music. Singers break into a section of yodeling as part of their song. Many jazz and hip-hop singers include a form of yodeling in their music.

25

DANCING

People dance to express their emotions during times of celebration, sorrow, or passion. In Europe, 20,000-year-old cave paintings show people dancing.

In hunting and gathering societies, people would dance before a hunt, to bring good luck and gain power over the animals. Other times they'd dance in celebration after the hunt, imitating the moves of the animals and thanking their spirits for their sacrifice.

Agricultural societies would dance to bring a good harvest or to ask for rain. Sometimes people danced during religious festivals or in celebration of a good harvest.

Break dancing started with street gangs in the Bronx in the early 1970s. Two dancers would

"Ghost Dancers" wore shirts painted with sacred symbols that they believed would keep them safe from bullets or arrows.

After a four-day buffalo dance, the people of the Native American Mandan tribe would share a bountiful thanksgiving feast to symbolize the early return of buffalo to Mandan hunting grounds.

prove their skills by trying to out-dance one another. These "battle dances" included martial arts moves and often were done as a substitute for gang violence. Unfortunately, sometimes the dances were so passionate they'd turn into real fights.

Couples in dance marathons during the Great Depression often competed simply to win enough prize money to feed their families for a while.

The Language of Life

Before writing, people used to hand down stories by word-of-mouth or through song. With the invention of writing, people started recording stories. They no longer had to rely on their memories. Anyone who could read could enjoy the story.

However, for thousands of years only a very small percentage of people knew how to read. Many rulers didn't know how to read either. They kept a **scribe** on staff to read and write important documents.

Storytellers traveled from place to place. For food and lodging, they entertained people with stories of history and religion, and of mythology and legends. In the process, they also spread knowledge. After they moved on, people repeated their stories and handed them down.

Early scribes wrote with a sharp stick on wet clay tablets. Later, the Egyptians invented **papyrus** to write on. In west Africa, people wrote on **parchment**.

The Chinese invented paper in AD 105, but its use wasn't common in Europe until 1200. The next great advance in books happened with Johannes Gutenberg's printing press in the 1450s. Up until that time, there were probably only about 50,000 books in all of

A Native American storyteller doll

Gutenberg borrowed money to survive while he developed his press. When he was within months of finishing the first printing of the Bible, for which he ultimately became famous, the money lender called in the loan. Gutenberg lost both his press and the Bible. His assistant, who married the money lender's daughter, finished the Bible. Gutenberg set up shop in another town, but he never cashed in on his wonderful invention. However, he earned his place in history with his press, for we know his name, while the money lender's and the assistant's names are forgotten.

Europe. By 1500, a mere fifty years after the press's invention, there were nine million books.

People read for pleasure as well as knowledge. In the future, electronic ink may lead to thin, flexible books, magazines, and newspapers with information that is updated through a wireless connection.

In the past, only free men knew how to read and write. It was against the law to teach women and slaves. In a remote area of China, though, women defied tradition and developed their own secret language. "Nushu," which means "woman's writing," was handed down from mother to daughter.

CONCLUSION

So many of the things we do today, people have done for thousands of years. Often their very survival depended upon how well they could hunt, or in Mesoamerica, on how well they could put a ball through a hoop.

In the future, people will continue to sing and dance, play games and read, because it is human nature to do so.

Our survival no longer depends on these skills, but our enjoyment of life certainly does.

Nothing says fun and relaxation like a good game of elephant polo!

Glossary

a cappella – singing without instruments

anthem – a song of praise or loyalty

aristocracy – a privileged group or family that rules a country

artifact – an object made by humans that is of historical interest

dressage – the guiding of a horse through complex maneuvers by slight movements of the hands, feet, and weight

edible – something that can be safely eaten

falconry – the art of using birds of prey such as eagles, falcons, hawks, and goshawks to hunt small animals and birds

fly – a fishing hook made to look like a small insect

Inuit – a specific group of Native Americans that live in the northern-most parts of North America and Greenland

Master Falconer – a person who owns and trains raptors, or birds of prey

Mesoamerica – the central part of the American continent extending from northern Mexico through Central America to Panama

metaphor – a figure of speech in which a word is used to describe something different from what it would normally describe. For example, "the evening of life" is a metaphor for "late in life."

migrating – moving seasonally from one place to another

outflank – to get around or avoid an opposing force

papyrus – a kind of paper made from the stems of the papyrus plant

parchment – a writing surface made from animal skins

scribe – a person who writes down what another person says

sentry – a soldier who is standing guard at a point of passage, such as a gate or a bridge

trawler – a boat used for pulling a large fishing net along the sea bottom

yeomen – independent farmers or lesser officials in a noble household

Index

Afghanistan, 13

Alexander the Great, 13

ancient Egyptians, 5, 8, 28

ancient Greeks, 5, 10, 14, 15

ancient Romans, 5, 23

bagpipes, 22–23

ball, 12, 13, 14, 16–17, 30

break dancing, 26–27

chariots, 8

Coubertin, Baron, 14

Darius III, 13

dressage, 10–11

drums, 22

equestrian, 11, 12

fishing flies, 4, 5

flutes, 22

Gutenberg, Johannes, 28–29

Haines, Jackson, 19

hip-hop, 25

ice skates, 19

immigrants, 25

International Olympic Committee, 14

Inuit, 20

Kamayura Indians, 22

Khan, Genghis, 12

King Harold II, 8

King Henry I, 9

King William II, 8

Mesoamerica, 14, 16–17

Olympic Games, 9, 11, 14, 15

printing press, 28-29

Richard the Lion-hearted, 8

roller-coasters, 21

skis, 18, 19

sleds, 20–21

spears, 5, 6, 8

Stone Age, 22, 24

stories, 25, 28

Tenth Mountain Division, 18, 19

toboggan, 20